Near-Death Experiences

NEAR-DEATH EXPERIENCES

Elaine Landau

The Millbrook Press ❑ Brookfield, Connecticut
Mysteries of Science

Library of Congress Cataloging-in-Publication Data
Landau, Elaine.
Near-death experiences / Elaine Landau.
p.   cm. — (Mysteries of science)
Includes bibliographical references and index.
Summary: Describes various categories of near-death experiences
and provides information about how scientists study unknown
phenomena.
ISBN 1–56294–543–2 (lib. bdg.)
1. Near-death experiences—Juvenile literature.   [1. Near-death
experiences.]   I. Title.   II. Series: Landau, Elaine.   Mysteries of
science.
BF1045.N4L36   1996
133.9′01′3—dc20   95–34026   CIP   AC

Published by The Millbrook Press, Inc.
2 Old New Milford Road, Brookfield, Connecticut 06804

For Illana Harkavi

Contents

The Near-Death Experience

More than twenty years ago Betty Eadie entered the hospital for routine surgery. The evening following the operation, while she was resting in her hospital bed, something unexpected occurred that changed her life.

It began with her growing extremely weak before drifting into unconsciousness. Then she experienced a quick bolt of energy as her spirit seemed to fly from her body. Suddenly, the woman felt as though she were hovering somewhere near the ceiling, and she was able to see her lifeless body on the bed below.

She soon found herself traveling through a dark tunnel. Yet she wasn't frightened; instead, she felt wonderfully content and calm.

Eadie then noticed a pinpoint of light glowing in the distance and began to move toward it. She described what it was like this way: "As I approached the light . . . I realized who the light was. Love emanated [came] from this being [of light] and his arms opened and embraced me. And I knew he was Jesus Christ. I said to him, 'I'm home. I'm finally home.' . . ."[1]

Betty Eadie described heaven as a splendid realm complete with beautiful waterfalls, brilliantly colored flowers, and wise guardian angels. She saw prayers float up from earth as beams of light. While there she also learned that "love is supreme" and that we are all born with a "divine, spiritual nature"[2] as well as an earthly body.

Eadie claims that she returned to Earth after being told that her purpose on earth had not yet been fulfilled. Although she was depressed over leaving paradise, Eadie looks forward to returning someday.

❑   ❑   ❑

Diane Morissey, a Los Angeles, California, office manager, says that she too has been to "the other side" and back. While at home cleaning her fish tank, Morissey was accidentally electrocuted. The force of the current propelled her head and shoulders through the living room wall. Morissey recalled her experience: "That's when I left my body. I couldn't control it. I couldn't make it not happen, and I didn't know why it was happening."

Diane Morissey felt herself drawn through a tunnel to a brilliant white light. Like Betty Eadie, she was deeply moved by the religious nature of her experience.

> I really felt the white light was God. . . . at that moment, I absolutely knew I was dead and . . . I felt I was given a choice to decide whether I was going to stay or come back. The paramedics thought that I was crying because I was in pain. But I was crying because I couldn't imagine that I'd picked to come back. I wanted to stay in the light. . . . A thousand words, all describing love, wouldn't come close to what the love felt like. [3]

Men and children have undergone similar experiences as well. While having surgery on November 7, 1979, Robert Helm went into cardiac arrest. Helm recalled going through a tunnel that had a bright light at its end. He heard music that he said was like "the sound of all the orchestras in the world playing with an intensity that was awesome." [4] He also felt a loving presence reaching out to assure him that everything was all right.

Helm passed through the light to find himself "sitting on a rock in the middle of a lake in the most beautiful location" he had ever seen. After that, he was transported to "a magnificent boulevard" and then to another place where a band of angels sang. Before leaving, Helm also visited a room containing a huge computer that he was allowed to use. When he finished at the keyboard he felt as if he had

"helped someone immeasurably."[5] At this point, Helm was told he would have to go back to his life on Earth.

After "returning" to his physical body, Helm told several people what had occurred. But only his wife believed him. Robert Helm feels that what he experienced profoundly changed him. He says that "now nothing seemed to be as impossible as it had before. . . . I'm not afraid of dying," Helm noted. "It is, without a doubt, the most wonderful experience I've ever enjoyed."[6]

❑ ❑ ❑

Children who have nearly died and remembered what it was like often describe these occurrences as a "weird dream." One researcher working with these young people said that a common response was, "Wow. It was really weird. I thought I was floating. I saw a light and there were a lot of good things in the light."[7]

Among the many youths who have had these experiences was sixteen-year-old Dean. Dean had suffered from serious kidney problems for some time. One day his parents brought him to the hospital when he had trouble breathing

---

Descriptions of near-death experience fall into several categories. Many reports include the presence of angels in a beautiful garden scene.

and had become confused as to where he was. They were in the hospital admitting room when Dean suddenly slumped down in his chair. A nurse rushed over to check the boy's pulse and found he didn't have one.

Hoping to revive him, the doctors used chest compression and drug injections to restart Dean's heart. Fortunately, they were successful, and before long the teenager was ready to go home. However, Dean left the hospital with some very unusual memories.

He later related what had occurred:

> I was apparently lying on a table in the intensive care unit when I suddenly found myself standing up and traveling through a very wide tunnel. . . . I knew there was something for me at the end of that tunnel, and I really wanted to get there. . . . Forget my body, forget being alive, all I wanted to do was to get to the end. . . . I reached a certain point in the tunnel where lights suddenly began flashing all around me. At this point I also noticed that there was somebody with me. He was about seven feet tall and wore a long white gown with a simple belt tied at the waist. His hair was golden, and although he didn't say anything, I wasn't afraid because I could feel him radiating peace and love.[8]

Like Dean, ten-year-old Chris also had a life-threatening kidney problem. After one of his mother's kidneys was transplanted into his body, the boy developed a low-grade

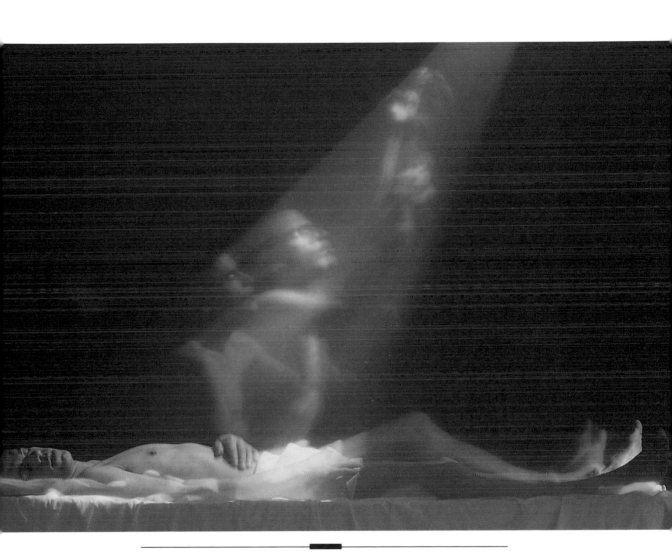

A physical experience of departing from the body is reported by many individuals who appeared to be dead. They describe a release from pain and a remarkable recollection of the efforts made to restore them to life.

fever his physicians couldn't control. When Chris began losing strength as the pain became unbearable, he entered the hospital.

Tests revealed that bacteria introduced into his body during the transplant had invaded his heart. To save his life, Chris's physicians performed heart valve surgery on him. While he technically "died" during the operation, the medical team managed to bring him back. Afterward, Chris remembered what happened:

> I'd been climbing a staircase to heaven . . . . I felt wonderful. I got about halfway up the staircase and decided not to go any higher. I wanted to go on up, but I knew I wouldn't come back if I went too high. That would hurt my mom and dad; since my little brother had already died, they wouldn't have anyone to take care of.[9]

Experiences such as those described here are usually pleasant and leave the person with a feeling of well-being. However, this isn't always the case. In a few instances, individuals who have almost died report seeing darkness rather than light and were terrified by beings more like demons than angels. Father Val Peter, director of Boys Town and a former theology professor, described such accounts: "I've spoken with people who were terrified. They spoke of darkness, cacophony [noise and discord], confusion, and a feeling of being lost."[10]

Nancy Evans Bush is the founder and president of the International Association for Near-Death Studies, Inc., in Windsor, Connecticut.

Researcher Nancy Evans Bush has spent years collecting reports of these unsettling experiences. She divided them into three basic categories. The first type is the experience in which the person is so upset that he or she views a basically positive experience negatively. Bush described it this way: "A person who approaches the light and is so fearful may see it as a reflection of the fires at the gates of hell, instead of seeing it as a radiant light."[11]

She summed up the second category as incidents where individuals experience "a great cosmic nothingness." They feel intensely alone and abandoned. In the third category, the last and smallest group of individuals believe they have been to an unending hell where inhabitants are continually tormented.

Both the good and bad episodes noted here are not as unusual as they may seem. Such incidents, in which clinically "dead" individuals are revived and go on to tell what "dying" was like, are known as near-death experiences, or NDEs. People have been fascinated by the possibility of life after death since the dawn of civilization. There is archaeological evidence that shows that the pharaohs of ancient Egypt had a keen interest in the afterlife. In the Middle Ages, popes sent priests far and wide to collect reports from those claiming to have caught a glimpse of the world beyond the grave.

Mormons, who strongly believe in life after death, have collected accounts of near-death experiences for more than

*The ancient Egyptians' belief in life after death
was so strong that they preserved the
bodies of their dead for use in the afterworld.*

150 years. And the Arapaho Indians of Wind River Reservation in Wyoming have a view of death that sounds strikingly similar to many near-death experience accounts. These Indians believe that as death approaches, the dying person must climb up a steep hill. On the distant side of the hill lies a village much like the person's own. The Arapaho believe that those who have already died wait there for the person, urging him or her to join them. On the near side are the dying individual's friends and relatives who beg the person

to go on living. The Arapaho think that sometimes people return from the hill. It might be a warrior wounded in battle or a woman who had difficulty in childbirth. Anyone could possibly survive and come back.

With advanced medical technology and mobile emergency units, more people are saved in perilous situations than ever before. As a result, the number of near-death experiences has skyrocketed in recent times. Researchers exploring the phenomenon estimate that at least one out of three people who survive a brush with death have a near-death experience. A Gallup poll further shows that more than eight million Americans claim to have had NDEs.

This book examines the remarkable similarities among near-death experiences and delves into the effect of NDEs on people's lives. Yet perhaps most importantly, the book explores the question of whether near-death experiences genuinely provide a look at life beyond the grave.

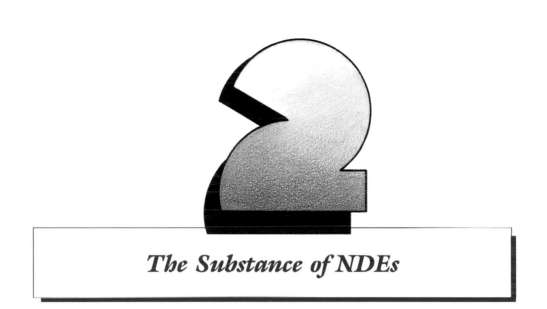

The Substance of NDEs

Studies show that while NDE reports often vary with the person's age, religion, and background, they are actually more alike than different. Dr. Raymond Moody is an Alabama psychiatrist who first identified and named the near-death experience. While Dr. Moody was initially skeptical of these occurrences, he eventually came to believe they were too numerous and similar to dismiss.

In researching NDEs, Dr. Moody isolated a number of characteristics common to most of these events. Although it is unlikely that any single person will experience all of these elements, NDEers usually cite several. Researchers suspect that the depth of the person's experience may be connected to the length of time he or she is clinically dead.

Some of the most commonly reported aspects of near-death experiences are listed below.

Finding it difficult to describe what they have been through. Many people who have had NDEs claim that there just aren't words to convey the intensity or full splendor of what they saw or felt. For example, one woman who had a near-death experience said, ". . . it was not like any light that's on earth. I mean colors like I've never seen, and I just can't describe them because there are no words for them. It's beyond technicolor."[1]

Another person who had an NDE following an automobile accident commented similarly: "The words aren't there to describe [it] . . . but everything was so vivid and so real."[2]

Hearing a doctor or other medical team member announce that he or she (the person having the NDE) *has died.* One woman scheduled for surgery went into cardiac arrest just before the operation. The physicians tried unsuccessfully to revive her. One of her doctors had said, "Let's try one more time and then we'll give up."[3] When the woman eventually regained consciousness, the only thing she recalled was hearing the doctor say that sentence.

Calm, peaceful feelings. Many people who have had NDEs report having feelings of love, well-being, and warmth at the time. Those in a great deal of physical discomfort prior to "dying" claim that all the pain and distress immediately vanished.

Strange sounds. Often those who have had near-death experiences say they heard unusual sounds or noises. In some cases, it may be an annoying whirling or buzzing. Other times, pleasant tingling bells or even beautiful music is heard.

Being outside their bodies. Large numbers of NDEers say they left their physical bodies and watched what was happening to them from a distance. Eight-year-old Michelle had an NDE after slipping into a diabetic coma. She spoke about leaving her body this way: "All of a sudden, I was floating above my body, looking down at myself. There were two doctors pushing me on one of those stretchers towards a room. Both were women doctors."[4]

In these situations, the person becomes a kind of spectator from on high. Some NDEers have repeated conversations that took place in other rooms that they couldn't have heard from where they were. Others cite incidents such as seeing a tray of operating instruments tip over that would have been impossible to observe from where they lay. Interestingly, blind people who have NDEs say they can see during these episodes. In such cases they have often been able to describe even small objects in various corners of the operating room.

Even though people having a near-death experience claim to have seen and heard what's going on, they are unable to interact with those around them. A patient interviewed by Dr. Moody recalled what it was like: "I saw them

resuscitating me. It was really strange. I wasn't very high. . . . I tried talking to them but nobody could hear me, nobody would listen to me."[5]

Seeing relatives and others who have already died. During an NDE, the person frequently sees a deceased parent, grandparent, or other individual who may have played an important role in his or her life. One woman was surprised when she was greeted by a small boy claiming to be her brother. As far as she knew she only had a younger sister who was still very much alive. When the woman later told her father about this, he looked astonished. It seems that he and his wife had a son years before the birth of their daughters. The sickly boy had died as a toddler and they never told the other children about him. The woman's father felt there was no way she could have known that she once had a brother.

The being of light. Among the most frequently cited elements in near-death experiences is seeing a being of light. This figure, who is sometimes viewed as God or a guardian

---

One of the most joyous experiences reported by individuals who have been near death is the perception of reuniting with deceased loved ones. This possibility offers particular comfort to mourners.

angel by these individuals, may serve as a spiritual guide on this special journey. The being of light is usually kind, loving, and accepting.

The life review. During an NDE some people see their lives pass before them. This stream of flashbacks begins with childhood, offering the person a chance to access how he or she spent the time on Earth. The NDEer is not condemned for any wrongdoings—the life review is solely for the person's benefit. "There was no one judging me," one woman said of her NDE life review. "I was judging myself. I saw thousands of bubbles, each containing an event in my life and I relived each scene. I could smell every smell and feel every emotion. . . . My whole life started to make sense."[6]

The reluctant return. Many NDEers claim they didn't want to return to their former lives and have their blissful experience end. Frequently, they say their spiritual guide told them their time hadn't come yet. Or that their work on Earth wasn't over. One nineteen year old recalled a group of faceless beings of light telling him, "You are not going

---

While most reports from those who have glimpsed life after death describe peace and tranquillity, religion has often viewed death as a time of struggle. The forces of good and evil wage battle over the departing soul.

to die. You are going back to earth. You have something to do."[7] When he asked what that was, the teen was told he would know when the time came.

Transformed lives. The majority of NDEers feel their experience dramatically changed them. Author and NDE researcher Dr. Melvin Morse believes that following a near-death experience, many individuals attach a greater purpose to their existence. He believes they have more zest for living than ever before. Carol Zaleski, Ph.D., a Harvard University lecturer on religion, agrees, adding that people who have near-death experiences appear to "gain wisdom."[8]

Such individuals also seem to become more adventurous. One research study on NDEs involved three separate groups: those who had NDEs, people who almost died but did not have NDEs, and others who had never come close to dying. Of the three categories, the individuals who had near-death experiences were more willing to take risks than both other groups. The researchers accounted for the results as follows: "The near-deathers were ready to go anytime. They tend not to be afraid of death."[9]

Kenneth Ring, Ph.D., a professor of psychology at the University of Connecticut, researched the long-range effects of NDEs. In surveying more than a hundred of these individuals, Ring identified measurable differences in their lifestyles following near-death experiences. For the most part, NDEers tended to appreciate life more. They developed greater concern and compassion for others and became less interested in material wealth and outward signs of status.

In summing up his conclusions, Ring wrote: "After [an NDE] the person can never again return to the former way of being. [The NDE] comes to take precedence over whatever he has been taught or previously believed. . . . It is not even just an experience that changes one's life. It *is* one's life. And it becomes the source of one's true being in the world."[10]

A case in point might be that of Barbara. Prior to her NDE Barbara described herself as a traditional housewife living in a well-to-do suburb. She indicated that in the past she and her husband had been very anxious to fit in with their friends and neighbors. However, following her near-death experience, Barbara felt that her real personality began to break through. Suddenly, she was no longer interested in what others thought of her. Now she just wanted to become the best person she could possibly be.

Barbara went back to school to train as a respiratory therapist. She said she wanted "to work with sick people," as she felt she "had so much love to give." Unfortunately, Barbara's new dedication came at a great personal cost. Her family and friends were unable to accept the changes in her, and her twenty-three-year marriage ended in divorce. But Barbara still felt she had made the right choice. "I left behind a lot of financial security," she noted. "But the spiritual security I was finding inside me was much more solid."[11]

Several independent studies revealed that near-death experiences may bring about other changes as well. There is some evidence that at times NDEers develop psychic abilities. "Following an NDE, people can often sense what someone is thinking, when someone is going to call, or when someone is about to die," reported Dr. Bruce Greyson, director of inpatient psychiatry at the University of Connecticut Medical School.

He also remarked that somehow the field of energy surrounding these individuals is altered. Dr. Greyson said:

> As incredible as it sounds, computers malfunction in their presence. Car batteries die. I don't know how many people have told me that streetlights have blown out, one by one, as they walked past them. The next stage of research will be to get people into the lab and measure their electromagnetic fields. [12]

Dr. Greyson further stated that some early evidence suggests that near-death experiences may also cause measurable physiological or bodily changes. It seems that numerous people who have had near-death experiences show long-term decreased blood pressure and pulse rates.

Dr. Bruce Greyson and Barbara Harris, a former colleague at the University of Connecticut. Behind them is a painting of the brilliant, yellow-orange light Harris described after her near-death experience.

NDEers who describe these changes to others often find that few people believe them. Instead, they are frequently regarded as highly imaginative, mentally unbalanced, or even godlike. An informal poll taken at an NDE support group meeting revealed that many of these people told no one about what happened to them for ten to twenty years. As one woman put it, "People either ridicule us or make us into saints. We've been zapped by something greater than ourselves, but we're still human."[13]

Near-Death Experiences—The Research

For many years the medical and scientific communities tended not to take the near-death experience seriously. Often dismissed as the rantings of delirious patients, some researchers felt that "a medical school bias [prejudice]" existed against it.[1] This meant little early funding for research, although in recent years attitudes have begun to change. With increasing numbers of similar near-death experiences reported around the world, fewer scientists doubt that these occurrences actually happen. Nevertheless, they do not necessarily regard NDEs as a gateway to paradise. Instead, many suspect that such events are a product of the mind rather than a true separation of body and spirit.

Researchers have proposed a number of possible explanations to account for near-death experiences. Some scientists point out that in stressful situations the brain produces natural pain-reducing substances known as endorphins. The scientists think that the extreme stress of dying may cause the endorphin level to rise to where the dreamlike state we call a near-death experience is produced. Many NDE reports, such as this one, fit that description: "Suddenly, amidst all this pain I saw a light, very faint and in the distance. It got nearer to me, and everything was so quiet. It was warm, I was warm, and all the pain began to go."[2]

Others think that NDEs might result from the decreased flow of oxygen to the brain at the time of death. Professor Susan Blackmore of the University of the West of England believes this oxygen deficit may account for the "tunnel" so many NDEers see. As the brain is deprived of oxygen during the last moments of life, its electrical system starts to fail, with cells firing frantically in every direction. In the portion of the brain responsible for vision, there are many more cells at the center than near the edges. As Dr. Blackmore stated: "Now imagine you've got lots and lots of cells firing in the middle, towards fewer at the outside. What's it going to look like? Bright light in the middle fading off towards dark at the outside. . . . that's where the tunnel comes from."[3]

Dr. Michael Sabom, a cardiologist and author on NDEs, feels such explanations don't account for what occurs. He argues that when the level of oxygen to the brain decreases, a person tends to become muddled and confused. In contrast, during an NDE, the degree of mental functioning and awareness is extremely clear. Sabom also doubts that NDEs are the result of an endorphin release. Endorphins relieve pain for 22 to 73 hours, he noted, while the NDEs are painless only as long as they last.[4] As soon as the person regains consciousness, any physical discomfort returns.

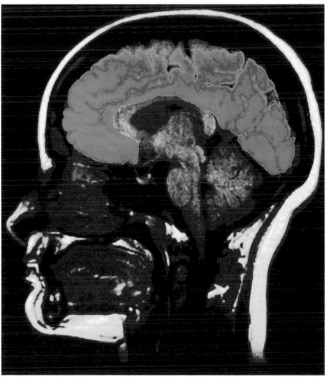

The ability to scan the brain with Magnetic Resonance Imaging (MRI) has made it possible to track brain activity during an NDE.

People have offered still other NDE explanations. Numerous scientists argue that similar reactions can be produced by stimulating certain parts of the brain. For example, stimulating the brain's right temporal lobe can bring about the life review frequently cited in near-death experiences. Stimulation of still another portion of the brain causes the person to see a very bright light. Some medical researchers suggest that the trauma of nearly dying triggers these brain reactions, causing the person to think he or she has been to heaven.

After studying near-death experiences, Ronald Siegel, an associate professor at the University of California at Los Angeles, noted that similar visions or hallucinations have also been sparked by fear, loneliness, or isolation as well as by certain "visionary drugs" such as LSD or hashish. Siegel further stresses that NDE-like episodes have already been induced in clinical trials through the use of various other drugs. "We can produce the fog, the tunnel, the light, and [the feeling of] an out-of-body experience," he reported. Siegel opposes the notion that NDEs are a journey to a spiritual realm. Instead, he believes that these experiences merely serve as "an adaptive [helpful] way for us to survive a life-threatening situation."[5]

The view of the near-death experience as a means of coping with possible death has also been suggested by psychiatrist Glen O. Gabbard, director of the C. F. Menninger Hospital in Topeka, Kansas. Gabbard observed, "This so-called out-of-body experience gives the person in a life-

*The NDE image of a bright light surrounded by
an aura can be induced by other psychologically
traumatic experiences as well, including drug use.*

threatening situation a chance to detach and be safe."[6] Distancing oneself from unpleasantness or stress has long been relied on by abused children in dealing with their difficult home lives. Interestingly, NDE researcher Kenneth Ring found an unusually high number of people who had near-death experiences were also abused as youths. Does this mean that abuse survivors are more likely to have NDEs? At this time, there isn't enough evidence to be certain of that.

A growing number of researchers insist that near-death experiences cannot be explained as either hallucinations or a way of coping with almost dying. They stress that hallucinations register on an electroencephalogram (EEG), a test measuring brain activity. But NDEers have had flat EEGs, making them appear to be brain-dead. These scientists also argue that most human experiences, whether it is falling in love, giving birth, or grieving, can be reduced to biological or bodily processes. However, that doesn't make them any less meaningful or real.[7]

A 1990 study at the University of Virginia in Charlottesville documented the spiritual aspect of NDEs. There, researchers interviewed fifty-eight people who had near-death experiences. Some of these individuals actually almost died, while others merely thought they were dying. Everyone interviewed reported seeing the light. However, only those who were genuinely close to death described the sense of peace and clear thinking characteristic of NDEs. "Physiological changes in the brain might account for the sensation [experiencing] of light, but not the mental clarity," stated Justine Owens, Ph.D., at the university's division of personality studies. "It appears that some spiritual experience was occurring."[8]

Other continuing NDE research includes the work of Madelaine Lawrence, Ph.D., who teaches at the University of Hartford, in Connecticut. Many of Dr. Lawrence's sub-

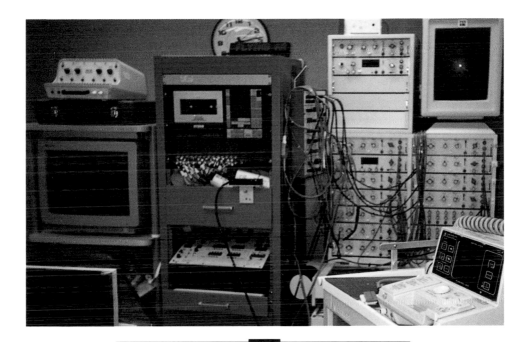

Dr. Madelaine Lawrence has devised a procedure to test the abilities of someone who claims to have left his or her physical body.

jects are hospital patients who were resuscitated after their hearts stopped. When interviewed, these patients often mention having had out-of-body experiences. Lawrence is trying to learn if these individuals actually left their bodies. As she put it, "Certainly, their perception is that they're out of their bodies. Whether, in fact, they are, that's one of the things we're trying to establish."[9]

In an experiment, she placed a sign bearing a nonsense message high on a cabinet. The sign was tilted so that you would either have to stand on a chair or be "outside your body" to read it. No one has correctly read the phrase yet, but researchers haven't ruled out the possibility that someone will be able to do so in the future.

❏ ❏ ❏

Despite the recent interest in NDEs, the bulk of the scientific community still remains skeptical. They argue that much of the research described as promising is actually anecdotal in nature—based on the stories of people claiming to have had NDEs. While anecdotal evidence certainly has some merit, scientists stress that it is a poor substitute for solid scientific data.

Doubting scientists further note that past scientific research stimulated by NDE stories has largely been shown to be inconclusive (neither proving nor disproving the theory tested) or negative.

Therefore, at this point, we still cannot be certain whether near-death experiences are a true bridge to the hereafter or, as most scientists suspect, merely a bodily response to dying. Perhaps as the phenomenon continues to be studied we may learn more. Meanwhile, the mystery of life after death remains a matter of personal belief rather than scientific fact.

Notes

Chapter One

1. ABC News *20/20,* "Embraced By The Light," Transcript #1419 (May 13, 1994).
2. Ibid.
3. ABC News *Turning Point,* Transcript #116 (June 8, 1994).
4. Robert Helm, "Glimpses of an Afterlife?" *Maclean's* (April 20, 1992), p. 38.
5. Ibid.
6. Ibid.
7. Nora Underwood, "Between Life and Death," *Maclean's* (April 20, 1992), p. 36.
8. Melvin Morse, M.D., *Closer to The Light* (New York: Villard Books, 1990), p. 29.
9. Ibid.
10. Robert T. Reilly, "Heaven Can Wait: Do Near-Death Experiences Take the Fear Out of Dying?" *U.S. Catholic* (January 1988), p. 12.
11. Nora Underwood, p. 37.

Chapter Two

1. ABC News *Turning Point,* Transcript #116 (June 8, 1994).
2. *Oprah,* "Flatliners: Near-Death Experiences," Transcript #1045 (September 13, 1990).
3. Raymond A. Moody, Jr., M.D., *Life After Life* (Harrisburg, Pa.: Stackpole Books, 1976), p. 27.
4. Nora Underwood, "Between Life and Death," *Maclean's* (April 20, 1992), p. 36.
5. Raymond A. Moody, Jr., M.D., p. 37.
6. Amy Sunshine Genova, "The Near-Death Experience," *McCall's* (February 1988), p. 104.
7. "The Music in the Light," *Maclean's* (April 20, 1992), p. 39.
8. Amy Sunshine Genova, p. 105.
9. Nora Underwood, p. 35.
10. Amy Sunshine Genova, p. 104.
11. Ibid. p. 105.
12. Ibid. p. 106.
13. Ibid.

Chapter Three

1. James Mauro, "Bright Lights, Big Mystery," *Psychology Today* (July/August 1992), p. 57.
2. Susan Blackmore, *Dying To Live: Near-Death Experiences* (Buffalo, N.Y.: Prometheus Books, 1993), p. 2.
3. ABC News *Turning Point,* Transcript #116 (June 8, 1994).
4. Amy Sunshine Genova, "The Near-Death Experience," *McCall's* (February 1988), p. 104.
5. Nora Underwood, "Between Life and Death," *Maclean's* (April 20, 1992), p. 37.
6. Alan Ebert, "A Glimpse of Heaven," *Redbook,* July 1991, p. 89.
7. Nora Underwood, p. 37.
8. Alan Ebert, p. 89.
9. ABC News *Turning Point,* Transcript #116 (June 8, 1994).

Glossary

archaeological—relating to the study of the remains of past human cultures

bacteria—various microorganisms that can be harmless and beneficial or virulent and lethal

deceased—dead

electroencephalogram—a test that records electrical activity in the brain

endorphins—natural pain-reducing substances produced by the brain

flashback—seeing or reliving an event or scene that occurred in the past

hallucination—seeing or hearing something that isn't there

near-death experience(NDE)—an occurrence in which a person believed clinically dead comes back to life and is able to relate what he or she experienced while unconscious

phenomenon—any unusual fact or occurrence

psychiatry—a branch of medicine concerned with mental and emotional health *psychic*—abilities outside the normal range of knowledge and senses

respiratory—related to the act of inhaling and expelling air; breathing

resuscitation—to revive or bring back from unconsciousness

stimulation—to stir or rouse

technicolor—a process used to produce especially bright, realistic color films

trauma—a physical injury resulting from considerable force or a severe emotional shock

Further Reading

Facklam, Margery, and Howard Facklam. *The Brain: Magnificent Mind Machine*. New York: Harcourt, Brace & Jovanovich, 1992.

Green, Carl R. *Out of Body Experiences*. Hillside, N.J.: Enslow, 1993.

Hamilton, Virginia. *In the Beginning: Creation Stories From Around the World*. New York: Harcourt, Brace & Jovanovich, 1988.

Krementz, Jill. *How It Feels To Fight for Your Life*. Boston: Little, Brown, 1989.

Parker, Steve. *The Brain & Nervous System*. rev. ed. New York: Franklin Watts, 1991.

Pringle, Laurence. *Death is Natural*. New York: Morrow, 1991.

Rofes, Eric E. ed., *The Kids' Book About Death and Dying: By and For Kids*. Boston: Little, Brown, 1985.

Stein, Sara B. *A Hospital Story*. New York: Walker & Co., 1984.

Index

About the Author

Elaine Landau received her bachelor's degree from New York University in English and journalism, and her master's degree in library and information science from Pratt Institute.

She has worked as a newspaper reporter, editor, and youth services librarian, and has especially enjoyed writing more than 85 books for young people.

Ms. Landau is in the best of health and has not acquired firsthand knowledge of a near-death experience.